How Living Things Help Each Other

Alice Reardon

Contents

Rigby

A Harcourt Achieve Imprint

www.Rigby.com
1-800-531-5015

What Are Living Things?

Animals and plants are living things.
All living things grow and change.
They need food, water, and air
to live.

How Do Plants Help Animals?

Animals eat parts of plants.

Many animals eat **seeds** and **fruits**.

Some eat **leaves** and stems.

Some animals live inside plants.
Some use leaves and grass
to make nests in trees.
Others use logs to make their homes.

Plants help animals stay cool and dry. They can also help animals stay safe from other animals. The color of plants can protect animals by making it hard to find them. Plants also help to make the air clean to breathe.

How Do Animals Help Plants?

Animals can help plants spread seeds.
Animals eat fruits that have
seeds inside them.
The animals take the seeds
away with them.
Sometimes other seeds will stick
to an animal's fur.
The animals bring the seeds
to new places.

Animals can also make the soil
better for plants.
Earthworms make tunnels in the soil.
These tunnels make it easy
for plant **roots** to grow.
Animal waste also helps plants.
It gives the plants food as it
breaks down into the ground.

How Can People Help Animals and Plants?

People can plant new trees and plants. These trees and plants will make more food and homes for animals. People can also work to keep the air, water, and land clean. All of this will help animals, plants and people, too!

WE
RECYCLE

Glossary

fruits

roots

leaves

seeds